I0791477

HAMILTON GITA

MUSINGS FROM THE ONE

HELEN HAMILTON

BALBOA.PRESS
A DIVISION OF HAY HOUSE

Balboa Press books may be ordered through booksellers or by contacting:

Balboa Press
A Division of Hay House
1663 Liberty Drive
Bloomington, IN 47403
www.balboapress.co.uk
UK TFN: 0800 0148647 (Toll Free inside the UK)
UK Local: 02036 956325 (+44 20 3695 6325 from outside the UK)

Print information available on the last page.

ISBN: 978-1-9822-8347-6 (sc)
ISBN: 978-1-9822-8348-3 (e)

Balboa Press rev. date: 04/22/2021

Contents

Dedication

I offer this book in the hope that it will inspire you and give you a glimpse of something amazing inside of you. You are that intelligence which gives light to all. These writings are a collection of lovingly written ramblings from the One. Let the power of your real Self read these words and lift you out of suffering and into peace.

My Beautiful Destruction

I have allowed myself to be deconstructed. I have been stripped bare to my core. I have untangled myself one by one from all the concepts I wore like garments.

I struggled initially to reveal myself. Allowing concepts to go seemed like a risk; but as each one went, I felt freer, lighter and safer. I felt encouraged and inspired to deconstruct more.

Each glorious layer of identity was given begrudgingly at first, then excitedly and some even fell away in my peace. Over and over again I saw this inter-tangled web of lies I had constructed around myself to be transparent and false.

Excitement turned to bliss and sheer joy at feeling my naked beingness once again. Unencumbered by the burdens of self-definition I let myself soar. Soon I began to search for more to discard; so absolutely smitten with the undressing of reality itself.

Everywhere I looked, I saw myself protected and guarded from my imaginary fears and shadows that vanished in the light. Bliss turned to ecstasy as I stumbled around my life begging to disrobe myself more. Sheer passion and love for my real nature inspired a closing down sale for my identity.

Deeper and deeper I dove into myself, revealing ever more subtle layers of ideas, projections and conceptions of myself. I had lost all remembrance of who I ever thought I was and I had lost all ability to want that back. I had lost any sense of loss and losing at all.

What started as sacrifice became a beautiful unveiling of the pristine state that I am. Lost in the revelling like some intoxicated nobody, I searched for more to throw away. Long ago had I lost the ability to value anything other than my own selfish drive inwards and downwards to the core of my own reality.

Finally in one ecstatic moment of blinding revelation, I gave away the ability to give away. I lost my ability to change, to become, to compare and to define myself. I ceased undressing and stood in front of the mirror of life. I recognised myself no matter how many concepts I wore.

I saw who I was before time and change came. I saw that I was also time and change.

I stood absolutely still for the first time and yet I had always remained right here.

A Moment and An Eon

I sit here alone, unaware of how long I have sat. Completely lost in myself I am no longer able to distinguish a moment from an eon. How many versions of me have come and gone whilst I was not looking?

I am utterly gone, lost and beyond all salvation and yet I am dimly aware of a time when salvation seemed important. Now it is an echo, a fading and fleeting insight into my many changing faces.

I appear as an atom or a universe and it moves me not. I dance endlessly as this play of light, life, creation and destruction. So enamoured am I with this never-ending parade of shapes that I lose myself in that. Each shape more beautiful than before until "more" and "before" also become just a shape for me to play with.

To some I am an idiot, a simpleton, so very gone from the world of normal and of expected; yet I know no such thing. If I have gone, then I am glad of it and I seek to destroy all passage back to the known.

I dared to flirt with the unknown and dived perilously deep into that ocean. I saw the known to be as insubstantial as

I am. I laughed deliriously at the idea that I could know something, or even know nothing.

Such beautiful illusion! Spinning endlessly out in front of me, I see all the ways I tried to confuse myself and then enlighten myself. Never ending amusement is all I amount to; a complete unfolding of joy.

Swimming in bliss, I desire to play again and again. Over and over again, I pretend to lose and then find myself again.

The microcosm reflecting the macrocosm; the microcosm appearing inside the macrocosm.

Is there but one playing? Or are there infinite games unfolding? I am so far beyond any ability to remember the answer.

A Prayer to Love

Let me see only myself.

Let me drink so deeply from this cup of truth, that only I remain afterwards.

Let me embrace all that I am until everything else is gone.

Let me forget me, you, this and that. Let me forget God, the world and the Self.

Let me forget everything I ever became.

Let me see the One in me, as me. Let me see myself revealed in every atom.

Let me keep nothing and yet hold everything in my embrace.

Let me drown totally and be reborn as new. Wash me clean and show me wonder, delight and joy.

Leave me open, exposed and defenceless to the love that you are.

Helen Hamilton

Let me lose all that never was and gain all that always is.

Let me see with perfect vision. Let me hear silence always. Let me bask in peace evermore.

I choose this, I am this. Let me always remember this.

Let my heart be pure.

Reverence to the One

Whom shall I worship now? Where shall I place my devotion? I find nothing to rest my attention on. I cannot find anyone to help me.

What do I give my reverence to now? What can I see that is unholy? There is nothing for me to release, remove or reject.

What should I practice now? Where do I need to go? There is nothing that I can become.

What can I possibly do now? There is nothing to be done or undone.

What is the use of surrender? There is nothing left for me to give.

The contemplator has vanished without a trace and there is nothing for me to see.

I have no need for goals, dreams or a purpose. I have no need for more, less or same. This fire has burnt everything and left nothing untouched.

What is the use in further imaginations?

Welcome Home

Welcome home to the Silence. Rest your head here weary traveller. How far have you come without taking one single step? How long have you walked just to arrive right back home?

For you see, you never left home and all of your wanderings were simply dream-like. Stay here with me and rest deeply. Drink deeply from this Silent place until you can wander no more.

Let each thought and each doubt rest here too; this Silence is large enough for everything to lay down and rest.

Bathe in this Silence until it has washed you clean of all imagination. Breathe in this Peace until it pervades you. Dive deeply into this Stillness until you forget how to leave.

Rest here with me and take off your shoes; you won't need them anymore. Stay here and forget everything, forget me and forget you. Silence is waiting to make you whole again.

There is nowhere else that you need to go.

Who Are You?

You created this entire universe and yet you never did anything.

You appeared as this human being and yet you were never born.

You sustain all this wonderful world and yet you never make any effort.

You are this ever-unfolding flower of manifestation and yet you have never changed or become anything.

You burn brightly as each star and yet you never burn out.

You think about yourself with every thought and yet you are completely silent.

Who are you?

You disturb yourself endlessly with your imaginings and yet you are ever peaceful.

You divide yourself again and again into two, many or billions and yet you are always just One.

You strive endlessly to be good enough and yet you are always perfect.

You ceaselessly explore and discover and yet there is nothing more to see.

You are always expanding infinitely and yet you have never grown.

You strive to reach home finally and yet you were always right here.

You have become this and that and yet absolutely nothing has happened.

Who are you?

You are this beautiful and yet inexplicable mystery and yet you are right here in plain sight.

You seek to know everything and yet you are all there is to know.

You are the One.

Look Again

Look again and see if there really is a world that you are moving around in.

Look again and see if there are any other beings except you. Search a little deeper and see if there is actually anything you want.

Inquire more deeply and find out if you are suffering.

Investigate fully and find out if you are missing out on anything at all.

Look closer at reality and see what it actually is.

Question again what there actually is for you to be afraid of.

Recognise completely that you are already free.

Question once more if you really have a mind at all.

Insist on finding out what you really are.

Be sure to find out if there actually are any phenomena.

Insist on discovering if objects are real.

Investigate completely if there is any manifestation at all.

Accept no limitations at all on your life.

I Forgot

I forgot this and that, here and there, now and then. I forgot everything I knew.

I forgot ignorance and knowledge; waking, dreaming and sleeping mean nothing to me.

I forgot to be enlightened or unenlightened, I don't know what liberation or bondage is.

I forgot how to seek, I forgot what I found. Nothing was worth keeping and everything was worth discarding.

I forgot I was worthy or unworthy. I forgot how to give or receive. Nobody was worth remembering and I have forgotten everyone.

I forgot I was lost and that I had arrived home. I forgot how to surrender and I found nothing at all worthy of my devotion.

I forgot to be finite or infinite. I forgot about lack or abundance. I found nothing worth keeping or having.

I forgot about you and I forgot about me. I forgot about everyone. I do not know what a relationship is.

I forgot the beloved and the lover. I forgot the Guru and the disciple. I found nothing worth holding on to.

Finally, I forgot how to remember and I forgot how to forget. I do not know what I have forgotten. I forgot everything and then I remembered myself.

Come Play With Me Here

I know you like to play hide and seek. I looked for you there and here. I looked for you yesterday and tomorrow. I tried to find you in the stars and the planets. I tried to discover you out there and in here.

I searched for you everywhere I could think of but I did not find you. I looked high and low and I travelled so far to find you. You had the best hiding place ever!

I looked for you in the Sages and Saints. I looked for you in the beggars and downtrodden. I looked for you in the scholars and philosophers. Still I could not find you. I know you like to hide right in front of me.

I searched for you in my dreams and my reality but I didn't find you. I looked for you in every experience I had but you were not there. I tried to think where you could be. I wandered through endless beginnings and endings to find you but still you eluded me.

I looked in my past and my future, I even searched my present moment and didn't see you. I tried to find your location but none was found.

Helen Hamilton

I know you like to play hide and seek. I know you like to hide everywhere all at once. I stopped looking for you and I found me. When I found me, I discovered you. I saw you had been hiding as me. I saw you playing as one, two and many.

I saw you everywhere and I saw you can never hide. What a beautiful game we played!

I Am Not in Your Concepts

I am not here or there; I am not now or then. I am not in the world, nor is the world in me.

I am not enlightened or unenlightened. I am not awake or asleep. I have no bondage or liberation.

I am not light or darkness. I have no vasanas or samskaras. I do no penance or practice.

I need no contemplation or meditation. I am not bliss or peace. No one can strive to reach me.

I am not beyond, inside or outside. I am not duality or non-duality. These mean nothing to me.

I have not transcended and I need no surrender. I am not devotion or prayer. You won't find me there.

I am not found in this lifetime or the next. I have no karma or evolution.

I am not found in attachment or detachment. They have no place for me. I am one and free already.

I am not time or timelessness. I am not form or formless. I am not silence or sound. All these are empty words.

I am not aware or unaware. I am not the waking, dreaming or sleep state. I am not beyond these either. I am not the fourth state.

I am not the ego or the Self. I am not found when two becomes One. You'll not see me there.

I am not action or inaction. I am not silent or noisy mind. Don't look for me there.

I have not manifested anything and I am not pure. I am not pristine or supreme. I am everything and nothing exists.

I am neither fear nor bliss nor am I the source of those. You will not see me there. I am not an achievement.

I am not austerities or holy rites. I am not found through practice and progress. I am not the future or the present.

I am not outside of concepts, nor am I inside them either. You cannot think about me or describe me.

I am not divisible or indivisible. I am not effortless or efforting. I have no work.

I am not tangible or intangible. Look deeper inside me. I do not take any shape, nor am I shapeless.

I am not one, two or many. I am not before or beyond anything. I am not anything at all. I am also everything.

I have no self-definition and I define myself as everything.

I have no eyes and yet I see it all. I have no ears and yet I hear myself. I have no hands yet I hold it all.

I do not move and yet I am all action. I do not need, yet I provide everything.

I am not making noise and yet I sound like existence. I do not speak, yet I never stop talking.

I am not bound and I am not free. I am nothing you can describe.

I cannot be believed in or conceived of. I am not imagination and I imagine this whole world.

I am before beginnings and after endings and I am moment to moment. I am birth, life and death.

All of this is nonsense. There is no path to reach me and I am at the end of every path.

You Are the Effortless One

You are effortless so stop trying.

You are already here so stop reaching.

You are already silent so stop making noise.

You are already free so don't reach for freedom.

You are infinite abundance so do not reach for more.

You are endless peace so stop trying to find it.

You are stillness and you don't need to move.

You have already arrived so stop trying to become.

You are not existence or non-existence so stop trying to go beyond.

You were never the opposites so don't try to put them down.

You are pure so stop trying to purify yourself.

You are the timeless One so don't reject time.

You are the light and you don't need to get rid of darkness.

You are already here so cease trying to arrive.

You were never lost and you cannot find yourself.

You are always the witness so stop trying to see.

Nothing is hidden from you so stop playing hide and seek.

You never forgot anything and you don't need to remember.

You are already everywhere so how you can find yourself?

You were never caught so don't keep trying to free yourself.

You have never been deluded so what use is enlightenment?

Portals to the Infinite

Stop making noise for a moment and you will hear silence. Cease the internal noise of desire and intention and you will hear yourself.

Stop travelling for a moment and you will find the end of your journey. No effort or change can make you be more you.

Don't try to come home and you will see you are already here. There are no steps you need to take.

If you stop trying to see, you will see clearly what you are. You are already the eternal witness of all.

Stop trying to find peace and it will find you instantly. You are only disturbed because you are trying to find peace.

Don't keep climbing and you will notice you are already at the summit of your being.

Stop making any effort for the moment and you will see you are the effortless One. There is no struggle for you.

Stop trying to be worthy enough and you will see you are the Supreme Reality.

There is no need to put yourself back together because you are already whole.

Stop searching for love and you will see you are the source of Infinite Love.

Don't keep agreeing that you need and you will have all that you could ever require.

Put down your desires for a moment and see you are already fulfilled.

Stop trying to get rid of your ego and you will see it was never really there.

Don't try to be more abundant and you will see there never was any lack at all.

Your efforts to be more expansive obscure you from seeing you are infinite.

Stop trying to find answers to your questions and all knowledge will reveal itself to you.

Just be still. Just be here with me.

You Are Everywhere and Not Somewhere

You were never just somewhere in time and space. You have always been everywhere. "Somewhere" and "someone" do not apply to you. "Location" and "existence" do not apply to you.

Come to see you are everywhere and you will see that no problems can affect you. All problems are to do with being somewhere in particular. No thoughts, issues or challenges for any particular body or mind can affect you because they are only relevant if you are somewhere.

You are formless and everywhere. Formless cannot have an edge or ending. Only forms can have an edge, size or an ending.

When you come to see that no thoughts and problems can affect you because you are everywhere, then those thoughts and problems will not affect your body or mind either.

All this duality is just a "seems to be". You are indeed everywhere but you also seem to be somewhere because your body appeared. When your body appeared you began to experience through those five senses. You began to think and remember and plan. Time began for you then. This is all just a "seems to be".

You are always everywhere and you have never been somewhere. You only seem to be somewhere in particular because of sense perception, thoughts and a sense of time and space. All these belong to the body. All these will go when the body goes. And then you will be as you have always been-absolutely everywhere.

You are here and you are not an object. So you are everywhere. Let the sense of duality play then. Let the "seems to be" of it all play. What is it to you? Nothing at all!

I Am Looking For the One…

I am looking for the one that will leave all thoughts alone.

I want to talk to that one who will leave all identity behind.

I want to see that one that needs no definition at all.

I would like to converse with that one who doesn't need or want anything.

I am looking for that one who values nothing.

I am looking for that one that questions everything.

I want to see that one that protects no corner of themselves from me.

I am looking for the one whose surrender is all encompassing.

I want to meet that one that gives everything up.

I want to find that one that sees all concepts are false.

I want to know that one that doesn't even want courage, faith or patience.

All This is Your Imagination Only

You don't have a body. It is made of pure space. You are never embodied or disembodied.

You don't have a mind; it is pure space. You are not bound or liberated.

There is no world; it is all the formless Self. You are never in the world or beyond it.

There are no other beings; you only imagine there are. You are everywhere all the time.

There are no problems for you at all so why keep imagining more?

There isn't anything to transcend or let go of. There really isn't a path to enlightenment. It is all in your imagination.

You are already free and pure, whole and indivisible like the sky. You never did manage to divide or merge. Unity and multiplicity are only in your imagination.

Destroy the Universe

There aren't any forms and nothing is really solid. There are no liquids, gases or solids. Destroy solid, liquid and gas now.

There isn't any object or thing at all. There isn't anything out there or in here either. Destroy out there and in here.

There isn't anything sentient or insentient; nothing animal, vegetable or mineral. Destroy these concepts too.

There is nothing alive and certainly nothing dead. Destroy birth, life and death too.

There is no time and timelessness. Destroy these concepts in your being now.

There aren't any enlightened beings or any unenlightened ones either. There is no freedom or bondage. Crush these ideas for me now please.

Somebody, nobody and everybody are pure fiction. Somewhere, nowhere and everywhere do not apply here. Destroy them now.

There is no I, you, he or she. There is no now, then or will be. There is no here, there or everywhere. What do you look like without these?

There is no separation, no unity, no merging and no realisation. There is only what always was.

There are no levels of consciousness and there isn't anyone left to reach them. There is no progress or resistance. All this is your imagination.

There is no Brahma, Vishnu or Shiva. Nothing is ever created, sustained or destroyed. There was no creation and there will be no dissolution.

There is no guru or disciple. There is nothing that went wrong. Nothing is hidden from you or revealed to you. Destroy these expectations now.

Nothing has happened to you and you did not fall from grace. You never were worthy or unworthy.

Nothing ever went wrong and nothing will go right for you. Just see clearly this is your imagination.

You have no karmic patterns, no tendencies at all. You have nothing to cleanse or purify. There are no vasanas for you and there is no good or bad karma for you.

You have never met another person and you never had a relationship. Destroy this too.

Only in your utter destruction will you realise your total completeness. Only when you are ready to destroy all you know, will you be able to see your true nature as the indestructible One.

What Must You Lose?

To see me, you must lose your comings and goings. You must lose your beginnings and endings. Set aside your one, two and many-ness.

To see me, it will cost you time and space. You must give up your difference and same-ness. I am very expensive because I will cost you everything and nothing.

To see me, you must sacrifice seeking and finding, becoming and arriving. You must also give up your allness and nothingness.

To see me, it will cost you God and Godhead, manifest and un-manifest. You must relinquish Self and ego too. I will make you lose everything.

To know me, you must lose your change and changeless. I will not be found in truth or illusion either. I will cost you everything.

To see me, you must let go of names, forms and the formless. I am not found in the transcendent and immanent either.

To love me, I will cost you creation and destruction. I will demand you let go of Brahma, Vishnu and Shiva too. I am not found in any of the realms or dimensions.

To know me, you must lose the teacher and the student. I am not found in the Sage or the disciple. I am not found anywhere or nowhere.

To see me, you must lose your duality and non-duality. I am going to cost you distinction and non-distinction.

To know me, it will cost you fear and hate. I will take from you guilt, grief and shame too. You must give me pride, anger and sadness. I will demand your ability to suffer. Give it all to me.

To know me, you must lose inside and outside, self and other. I am very expensive because I will cost you Self and not-Self too.

I will cost you everything that you can think of. I am very expensive. I will take everything that you have and all that you have become.

Do not be scared of me even though I will cost you everything; for I will give you so much more. Know me and I will give you yourself. I will give you safe haven. I will give you immortality. Find me and you will find your home and your indestructible peace.

There is no need for fear for I am already here. Come and see me and see your real face!

I Want to Show You YOU

I want to show you what you really are. I want to show you the perfection that always is. I want you to notice how perfect you are and have always been.

I want you to see You, but you must look without your concepts.

I would love to show you wholeness beyond division. I would rejoice in you seeing your infinite nature beyond any sense of limitation.

I want you to see the real You, but you must look without your ideas.

I want to show you wonder, splendour and infinite wisdom that is already yours. I would like you to recognise your timeless and deathless Self.

I want you to see the real You, but you must look without your doubts.

My heart longs to show you your true beauty. You are glorious and spectacular and better than you can ever imagine.

I want you to see the real You, but you must look without any self-definition.

I want you to know with conviction that you never began and will never end. I want you to see the universe appearing inside you.

I am your mirror and I want you to look at yourself clearly. You just need to look without mind.

I want to show you how free you already are. I want you to see you never had anything to do. I want you to know that you were never lost or found.

I want you to see the real You, but you must be willing to see your already-so perfection.

I want to show you that you have never been a traveller and that all roads home appear inside you. I want to show you that you never moved at all.

I just ask for one chance to show you Yourself. I just long to show you completeness. I wish I could tell you the great importance of seeing. But I simply sit in my own peace, ever watchful for that moment that you are willing to look. Whenever you are willing to see, I will take some shape to show you. Whenever you are ready to look, I will take some form to guide you. You will never be abandoned.

The Glory of Being Wrong

In the end, this is the highest attribute of all. It is the most worthy one of all who is wrong about everything. I want that one who is willing to be wrong and to see that nothing we have imagined or conceived about ourselves is true.

Oh the glory of being wrong! The joy of knowledge collapsing! The release of burdens carried is exquisite! I want that one who is ready to be totally wrong. Come and bathe in the bliss of not knowing with me. Come and sit in the unending peace with me. Feel your imagined limitations drop away as you see your true face.

Yes! The glory of being wrong is the gateway to Nirvana. Life's wonderful paradox is that the least sought after experience is the most valuable one of all. The ego hates being wrong but the Self longs for it. Being wrong is the highest of all. The ecstasy of being totally wrong about everything we imagined to be is so total and complete that you will want to feel it again and again.

May the One save me from ever being right about anything! Come and be totally wrong with me. I welcome you into my home but you cannot bring anything other than yourself.

Truly, everything you believe has held you back is imagined. All your suffering is in your dream only. Wake up by being wrong-just be willing to be wrong. That's all I ask of you. Don't cling to any idea about yourself, me or anything at all for a moment.

What if all concepts are untrue? Wouldn't you like to know? I want to pull all these ideas out of you and set you free. Each and every thought you believe is causing you pain. You are dreaming all these limitations. You are dreaming all these lifetimes. You are imagining all these beings. Come and play here with me. There is only one price to pay for freedom; you must be willing to be wrong about how far you have come.

The One is sleeping and dreaming all these fantastic galaxies, worlds and amazing lifetimes as a human being. You have endless and infinite dreams about characters who never really were at all. Squeeze yourself through the small hole in your dream — the urge and pure desire to be wrong. Oh how wonderful!

Be free of your own self-made prison and rejoice in your total and utter clarity. Be wrong about everything and be home instantaneously with me.

If I Could Only Show You…

If I could only show you for a moment what it is like to be me, you would immediately surrender all your resistance to love.

If I could only show you what it is like to have forgotten how to feel bad, you would dive right into the true state.

If I could only show you for a second how it feels to be unable to argue with what is, you would give up all your arguments with yourself, God and everything right now.

If I could make you feel even just for a moment, the unending and ever deepening peace, love, joy and bliss that I feel every moment, you would not waste any time tolerating untruth.

If you could watch through my eyes as problems and amazing solutions appear spontaneously, then you would want to see it the same way I do.

If I could show you how it feels to be completely unable to resist, to suffer or to fear ever again; then you would walk straight ahead into Reality.

If I could show you just for a second how it feels to know you can never run out of anything, then you would realise your infinite abundance.

If you could feel adequate, complete and worthy, just as I feel in every moment, then you would go beyond any self-doubt.

If I could only show you how it feels to desire nothing at all in this moment, then you would not even desire Truth anymore.

If I could only show you in this moment, what it is like to be awake to Reality, you would spontaneously wake up right now.

If you could only feel for even a moment, what the complete absence of fear and loss feels like, then you would drown in bliss right now.

If I could somehow give you my experience in this moment, then you would know peace and love that are always on the edge of being too much to deal with. You would know an ever-deepening capacity to love.

If I could only show you how it is to know nothing at all, you would immediately forget all your knowledge and your ignorance.

If I could only show you how it feels to help every single being you encounter, just with your Presence, you would immediately want to resonate and radiate that Presence completely.

If I could only show you how complete it feels to be home right now in this moment, you would absolutely stop your journeying.

If somehow I could show you how it feels to know completely that you are loved, wanted and worthy, then you would know your value has never been in question at all.

If I could only show you for a moment what it is like to be me, then you would know what it is like to be you!

I cannot show you at all and I cannot give you my experience either. All I have is my Presence and my words to try to inspire and encourage you and that is enough. All I can give you is the example of what I am and that is enough. All I can give you is my authenticity and my Reality.

Let these words light a fire in you and let your heart burn with desire to feel how I feel. Don't allow anything to stop you until you experience what I do in every moment. Become a living manifestation of these words and fulfil my desire for you to see your own greatness.

The Greatest Freedom Of All

The greatest freedom of all is to be who you are. I want you to be who you are; not who you want yourself to be or who you think you should be. Be exactly who you are and not who you have been taught to be.

The greatest freedom of all is to be exactly as you are in each moment. If you find yourself lost in thoughts in this moment, be completely lost. If you find yourself completely aware of nothing at all, then be totally aware of that. If you are distracted by a noise, sensation or an ache, then be completely distracted right now.

Making no effort to control or change anything at all is the greatest freedom of all. Being completely at peace with what is right now is the greatest freedom. To be totally unable to "should" or "shouldn't" about yourself or anything is the most beautiful way to be.

Whatever you think you are doing is being done by your body. Whatever you think you are thinking is being thought by your mind. Wherever your attention wanders is wherever your attention wanders. None of this is anything you must or can control.

The greatest freedom of all is to be exactly as you are in this moment. Just relax and don't try to control or change anything about this moment and you will come to see that nothing needs to change after all.

The only thing you shouldn't do is to believe in "shouldn'ts". Allow everything its authenticity in each moment and let go of holding on. Be completely accepting of how things are right now. If you feel bad then feel bad. If you feel good then feel good. Peace comes from acceptance and not necessarily liking what is. When you accept what is, then what will be begins to please you greatly.

Most of all — give yourself the total freedom to be completely unenlightened in this moment. Even if you feel you should be more awake, then give yourself permission to feel that fully. When you *finally* come to be exactly as you are in this moment, you will be authentically awake right now. You will be perfect in your imperfections. You will have arrived, even whilst still trying to get there. You will be a living example of the greatest freedom.

I Love You Too Much

I love you too much to think about you. I won't sully you by assuming anything of you or about you. I won't burden you with any expectations or demands. I'd like to meet you as you are.

I love you too much to separate you from me. I won't impose any distance at all on us. I won't tolerate the distance of thoughts between us. I want to meet you exactly as you are.

I love you too much to believe anything about you. I don't care to project onto you. I respect you too much to know anything about you. I won't limit you that way. I want to meet you in your authenticity.

I love you too much to label you or categorise you. I will not allow thoughts to define and shape my experience with you. I prefer to meet you exactly as you are.

I love you too much to ever know you or understand you. I care too deeply to have a relationship with you at all. Such distance of two is too much for me. I cannot bring myself to externalise you. I want to meet you just as you are.

I love you too much to try to define you. I won't allow any restriction on you at all. I don't care to imagine how you are and I don't want to remember you ever. I want to meet you exactly as you are.

You see, I love you too much to think about you at all. I love you so much, I forgot about you and I forgot about me. All that is left then, is the pure experience of being and meeting each other exactly as we are. How amazing to meet you with no barriers at all!

I Want Never Gets

It's true, I want never gets. You won't get what you want at all. You won't wake up and you won't reach nirvana.

I want never gets, "they" say. Perhaps "they" knew the truth after all. Whoever "they" are must have known that "I want" is never going to happen.

You want enlightenment. You want peace and you want to be the One Being. But your desire is only a reflection of the One wanting to recognise itself.

You see, the feeling "I want" is really how a human body and mind feels when it is used by the One Being to help it consciously recognise itself.

Yes! "I want" is a symptom of an awakening that is already well under way. Under the surface of "me" and "mine" big changes are happening.

"I want to wake up" is the last call of this dream character, as the great dream of the One comes to an end.

"I want to wake up" is a sign or an indication of an awakening that is nearly complete. Sadly, for this dream character, we find that "I want never gets". But for you, the One Being, "I want" becomes "I Am".

And in the end "I want" never getting is the greatest joy of all. Nothing is left to fulfil or reach. Just absolute peace and quiet. The "I" that wanted has simply vanished into the Great One; seen clearly to have never been anything more than the last remnants of a vivid imagination.

Empty Yourself Now

Empty yourself out now and stay like that with me. There is nothing at all worth keeping. It is not worth being sad, frightened, angry, jealous or prideful just to have some self-definition.

Empty yourself out now of all self-defining concepts and rest there. It is not worth being someone, being nobody or even being the Self. Rest without any definition at all.

Do you really need to understand yourself more? Will this really bring you peace? All realisations and epiphanies must go also. Knowledge and ignorance must go. It is not worth keeping anything at all.

Empty yourself out now completely and see how that feels. Have nowhere to stand at all. It is not worth feeling you were born and will die, just to have some self-definition. It is not worth feeling that anything at all happened when this body came.

Empty yourself out of all the things you think you have acquired; they are only ideas. Nothing came to you and you will lose nothing. It is only you. You remain as you are, before all of this.

If you would like more information about
Helen Hamilton, her live Satsangs,
silent retreats and classes please contact us:

❖ Our website is www.helenhamilton.org

❖ Find Helen on Facebook by searching:
   @satsangwithhelenhamilton

❖ Email us at evolutionofspirit@gmail.com

❖ Search for us on You Tube at satsangwithhelenhamilton